MW00607602

I dedicate this book, first of all, to my wife, Cindy, who thought of the idea and granted me the time to bring it to fruition.

To my sister, Jill, who is my encourager and cheerleader.

To my granddaughters, Leah, Anna, Elle and Abby, who I hope will one day turn and become children of God.

Finally, to my Savior and Lord, Jesus Christ; for apart from Him, I can do nothing (John 15:5).

BIBLE
The Bible tells me...

...there is a God.
Genesis 1:1

...God created the heavens, the earth
and every living thing.
Genesis 1

...God is in heaven.

In Heaven,
there is no sadness or crying,
no pain, no sickness and no death.

Isaiah 66:1; Revelation 21:3,4

BFFs
BFFs
...God desires to be my BFF.*
Psalm 25:14; John 15:12-15;
Revelation 21:3
*Best Friend Forever

...God is great.

...God is all-powerful,

all-knowing

and everywhere.

Psalm 48:1; Jeremiah 51:15; Psalm 147:5; 2 Chronicles 16:9

... only God is good.
Psalm 25:8; Luke 18:19
to: you
♥: Go
BIBLE
GIFTS
the WAY
fruit of the Spirit
family
friends
life

...I am NOT good because I sin.
Sin is NOT God's Way.
Psalm 14:1-3; Romans 3:23

...God does NOT sin.

Isaiah 6:3; Revelation 4:8

...God showed His love
by making me unique.
No one is exactly like me.

God has a special purpose for me.

Psalm 139: 13,14; Jeremiah 1:4,5

...Jesus is God in human form.
Matthew 26:63,64; John 1:1-5,14

Jesus gave His life for me so that He can be my BFF.*

John 3:16,17; John 15:12-17

*Best Friend Forever

...on the cross, Jesus died in my place.

Romans 5:8,9

...on the cross, Jesus conquered sin for me.

Romans 6:10,11

...on the cross,
Jesus conquered death for me.
Romans 6:23

...Jesus
rose from
the grave,
so I can have
new life in
Him.
1 Corinthians
15:1-9;
Revelation
1:17,18;
Romans
8:11

...I must TURN from going my way to going God's Way.
Matthew 18:1-3
Ezekiel 18:30
FOG AHEAD
U-TURN NOW
MY WAY
GOD'S WAY

...I must BELIEVE in Jesus.

John 1:12,13

...I must RECEIVE Jesus into my life and follow Him.
Matthew 16:24

...I must RECEIVE Jesus

into my actions,

into my thinking,

into my emotions

and into the choices I make.

John 1:12,13

...if I TURN,
BELIEVE
and RECEIVE Jesus,
then I will become
a Child of God.
John 1:12,13

...only a Child of God
can have Jesus as a BFF.*
I John 3:1-10
*Best Friend Forever
BFF's

...only a Child of God can be with Jesus in heaven.

Matthew 18:1-3

...only a Child of God
can have God's Spirit living
inside one's heart forever.
John 14:15-17

...Jesus is coming back!
John 14:1-3; Revelation 22:7
GLORY
Our Lord COME
1 CORINTHIANS 16:22

Bible Verse References *(from the ESV, English Standard Version)*

Pages 2, 3: In the beginning, God created the heavens and the earth. -Genesis 1:1

Page 4: Thus says the Lord: "Heaven is my throne, and the earth is my footstool; what is the house that you would build for me, and what is the place of my rest? -Isaiah 66:1

And I heard a loud voice from the throne saying, "Behold, the dwelling place of God is with man. He will dwell with them, and they will be his people, and God himself will be with them as their God. He will wipe away every tear from their eyes, and death shall be no more, neither shall there be mourning, nor crying, nor pain anymore, for the former things have passed away." -Revelation 21:3-4

Page 5: The friendship of the Lord is for those who fear him, and he makes known to them his covenant. -Psalm 25:14

"This is my commandment, that you love one another as I have loved you. Greater love has no one than this, that someone lay down his life for his friends. You are my friends if you do what I command you. No longer do I call you servants, for the servant does not know what his master is doing; but I have called you friends, for all that I have heard from my Father I have made known to you." -John 15:12-15

And I heard a loud voice from the throne saying, "Behold, the dwelling place of God is with man. He will dwell with them, and they will be his people, and God himself will be with them as their God." -Revelation 21:3

Page 6: Great is the Lord and greatly to be praised in the city of our God! -Psalm 48:1

It is he who made the earth by his power, who established the world by his wisdom, and by his understanding stretched out the heavens. -Jeremiah 51:15

Great is our Lord, and abundant in power; his understanding is beyond measure. -Psalm 147:5

For the eyes of the Lord run to and fro throughout the whole earth, to give strong support to those whose heart is blameless toward him. -2 Chronicles 16:9

Page 7: Good and upright is the Lord; therefore he instructs sinners in the way. -Psalm 25:8

And Jesus said to him, "Why do you call me good? No one is good except God alone." -Luke 18:19

Page 8: The fool says in his heart, "There is no God." They are corrupt, they do abominable deeds; there is none who does good. The Lord looks down from heaven on the children of man, to see if there are any who understand, who seek after God. They have all turned aside; together they have become corrupt; there is none who does good, not even one. -Psalm 14:1-3

For all have sinned and fall short of the glory of God. -Romans 3:23

Page 9: And one called to another and said: "Holy, holy, holy is the Lord of hosts; the whole earth is full of his glory!" -Isaiah 6:3

And the four living creatures, each of them with six wings, are full of eyes all around and within, and day and night they never cease to say, "Holy, holy, holy, is the Lord God Almighty, who was and is and is to come!" -Revelation 4:8

Bible Verse References *(from the ESV, English Standard Version) continued...*

Page 10: For you formed my inward parts; you knitted me together in my mother's womb. I praise you, for I am fearfully and wonderfully made. Wonderful are your works; my soul knows it very well. -Psalm 139:13-14

Now the word of the Lord came to me, saying, "Before I formed you in the womb I knew you, and before you were born I consecrated you; I appointed you a prophet to the nations." -Jeremiah 1:4-5

Page 11: But Jesus remained silent. And the high priest said to him, "I adjure you by the living God, tell u if you are the Christ, the Son of God." Jesus said to him, "You have said so. But I tell you, from now on yo will see the Son of Man seated at the right hand of Power and coming on the clouds of heaven." -Matthew 26:63-64

In the beginning was the Word, and the Word was with God, and the Word was God. He was in the beginning with God. All things were made through him, and without him was not any thing made that wa made. In him was life, and the life was the light of men. The light shines in the darkness, and the darkness has not overcome it. -John 1:1-5

And the Word became flesh and dwelt among us, and we have seen his glory, glory as of the only Son fror the Father, full of grace and truth. -John 1:14

Page 12: "For God so loved the world, that he gave his only Son, that whoever believes in him should not perish but have eternal life. For God did not send his Son into the world to condemn the world, but in order that the world might be saved through him." -John 3:16-17

"This is my commandment, that you love one another as I have loved you. Greater love has no one than this, that someone lay down his life for his friends. You are my friends if you do what I command you. No longer do I call you servants, for the servant does not know what his master is doing; but I have called yo friends, for all that I have heard from my Father I have made known to you. You did not choose me, but I chose you and appointed you that you should go and bear fruit and that your fruit should abide, so that whatever you ask the Father in my name, he may give it to you. These things I command you, so that you will love one another." -John 15:12-17

Page 13: But God shows his love for us in that while we were still sinners, Christ died for us. Since, therefore, we have now been justified by his blood, much more shall we be saved by him from the wrath c God. -Romans 5:8-9

Page 14: For the death he died he died to sin, once for all, but the life he lives he lives to God. So you als must consider yourselves dead to sin and alive to God in Christ Jesus. -Romans 6:10-11

Page 15: For the wages of sin is death, but the free gift of God is eternal life in Christ Jesus our Lord. -Romans 6:23

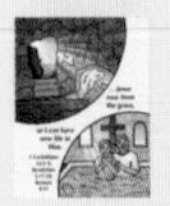

Page 16: Now I would remind you, brothers, of the gospel I preached to you, which you received, in which you stand, and by which you are being saved, if you hold fast to the word I preached to you—unles you believed in vain. For I delivered to you as of first importance what I also received: that Christ died for our sins in accordance with the Scriptures, that he was buried, that he was raised on the third day in accordance with the Scriptures, and that he appeared to Cephas, then to the twelve. Then he appeared to more than five hundred brothers at one time, most of whom are still alive, though some have fallen asleep Then he appeared to James, then to all the apostles. Last of all, as to one untimely born, he appeared also to me. For I am the least of the apostles, unworthy to be called an apostle, because I persecuted the churc of God. -1 Corinthians 15:1-9